THE 5 ACTIONS

5 Simple Actions That Will Take Your Business, Marriage,
Friendships, and Overall Life to the Next Level

KWANSI COOKE

THE 5 ACTIONS

TABLE OF CONTENTS

Acknowledgments

There are so many people I could thank. I would like to start with my ancestors and spirit guides for guiding me down this path of helping others to unlock their full potential. I want to thank my wife, Nichole Cooke; my parents, Sean and Roxanne Cooke; and my sisters, Shabika, Cashmere, and Toshawna Cooke. They all played a pivotal role in helping to groom the man you will read and learn about throughout this book.

Even though the people above helped groom me, there isn't a single "who" I can directly thank for helping me publishing this book; it is actually a compilation of "whats." This book was fueled by an assembly of events that took place throughout my life. All of the ups and downs helped and motivated me to write this book. So I would like to thank this journey we all call *life*. Everything I have endured has helped me write this book to, in turn, help others avoid the countless hurdles I faced to get to where I am now.

TODAY'S PROBLEM

In today's society, everything is all about instant gratification and quick results. It doesn't seem many people are interested in putting forth the time, effort, and work required to reach their true potential. However, the issue with quick results is they never seem to last and never are as satisfying. Anything worth having always requires time and effort. It takes research, mistakes, and actions to see desired results. Everyone in this world is destined for some level of success. My level of success is completely different from the next person's. Some people measure success by how much money and fame they can acquire, while others deem companionship, family, and helping others as the ultimate success.

For someone to determine how they measure success for themselves, they will need to dig deep within. Digging deep within means searching and *re*discovering your thoughts, feelings and beliefs regarding something to get to know yourself on a deeper level. The problem many face when digging deep is cognitive dissonance. *Cognitive dissonance* is mental discomfort when someone holds two conflicting beliefs, values, or attitudes. When this happens, it creates chaos and stress within a person. One must choose one side or the other to calm the chaos.

When met with cognitive dissonance while rediscovering what can work in our lives, one must let go of the fear of contradicting themselves. Growth happens when we've decided that we're tired of the same results and choose to change something and head in another direction—usually a more positive one. Let's look at an example of this: Someone wants to lose weight. Most people know that working out can help them lose weight. If you run every day, you may lose weight, but if you do not change up the routine, you will ultimately hit a ceiling. Now, this does not mean running is wrong; it just means you'll have to grow if you want to reach new heights of fitness. It's time for you to find and utilize newfound knowledge.

The same is true when you want to enhance your everyday life. If you give the same answer to the same question six to twelve months later, you simply haven't grown. You should always strive to attain new knowledge. Even if your stance on a subject hasn't changed, your view on the subject should. Growth encompasses the ability to change our views based on newfound information that has been acquired through triumphs and lessons.

Questioning or adding to our past answers or beliefs does not mean we are contradicting ourselves; it means we have humility and are magnets for ascension.

INTRODUCTION

Who am I? This is a very valid question. I am no different from you. Now, you may be thinking, "If you're just like me, how are you supposed to help me?" The answer is rather simple. My name is Kwansi Cooke, and the reason I consider myself no different than you is that, in one way or another, we have all been trapped in a state of mind where it feels like our life is on a treadmill. Even though we are putting forth effort, we seem to be standing in the same spot, mentally, financially, and spiritually. Because I have felt just like you and took the leap of faith to get uncomfortable, I thought to myself, "If this process helped my life soar to new heights I didn't know were obtainable, how can I map it out to help others?" With time and effort, many trials and errors, I boiled my experience down to just five action steps that you'll read about soon.

I was born in Newark, New Jersey, and raised in East Orange, New Jersey. Both locations are universally known for having broken homes, being infested with crime, and lacking access to positive role models that can help people succeed. I have served in the army for eleven years, with two tours on foreign soil. I have been deployed to both Afghanistan and Kuwait. I am also happily married; however, this is my second shot at it, haha.

I highlight these parts of my life because all of my experiences, the good and bad, have helped me create these five steps that have proven effective in real-life events. As a result of the trials and tribulations I have faced, I am now an author, a successful public speaker, and the owner of a real estate investment company, and I have a prosperous military career. As I walk you through each of these five steps, you'll be able to reach the same heights as I have, no matter the cards you were dealt. So sit back, find a comfy spot, grab a highlighter and something to takes notes, and block out the *outside* world, so you may repair your *inside* world, which will ultimately reflect in your current reality.

Action 1

Change the Angle, Change the Picture

There are no two people on this green earth that are the same, not even identical twins. You can have siblings that grew up in the same house as you, shared the same experiences as you, and were taught the same things as you and still be complete polar opposites. Isn't it fascinating how you can have all of these common denominators yet have different reactions to the same experiences? The reason behind this all comes down to a matter of perspective. By definition, *perspective* is basically a particular attitude about someone or something. To simplify that, it is your *point of view*, and we all know that everyone has their own point of view and opinions on various topics and situations. Now let's explore the power of perspective. When you change the perspective, you inevitably change the picture. Let's take a minute to try an exercise I've tested on several different individuals. I want you to stand outside, extend your arm and place your palm toward your face so that it is directly level with your head and eyes. Take a moment to reflect on what you see. What do you see? Most people immediately notice their hands, fingers, nail polish, rings, bracelets, and anything else that may be associated with their hand or wrist.

Now let's break this down. The experience was placing the hand in front of the face, which was the same for every individual, but the reaction, which is what people chose to see, was different. The biggest highlight of this experiment is that everyone that participated chose to focus on their hand, when they weren't instructed to do so. Everyone failed to identify trees, cars, grass, and basically everything else that was happening beyond the hand in their face. This is because people's perception has been nurtured to focus exclusively instead of inclusively. We tend to forget about the bigger picture and focus on the smaller details. When changing our perspective, it is important to include everything to get a better understanding with all variables.

As a leader in the United States Army, I've had the privilege of being accountable for the well-being of several soldiers at a time, which is no easy task. At once, I can be in charge of up to six subordinates. The majority of the time, these soldiers come from different backgrounds and geographical locations, and all with their own perspectives based on their upbringing. It is imperative that I, as their leader, can change my perspective and angle to see the whole picture and acquire all of the variables before making decisions. This requires me to utilize the ability to see more than just my hand, as all perspectives and angles in the "photo" have to be accounted for to make informed decisions that are fair and impartial.

There's a popular saying in the military: "If you're on time, you're late, and if you're early, you're on time." Clearly, someone who had nothing better to do with their time is the author of this saying, haha, but as I mature, I understand the concept behind it. In reality, however, this quote has become a mantra that every military member abides and lives by. In 2013, I had the privilege of being stationed in Germany, and I was in charge of four soldiers. On a particular day, there was an important ceremony every soldier in the battalion was required to attend. The ceremony was set to begin at 3:00 p.m., so I requested my soldiers show up at 2:50 to ensure we would start on time. At 2:55, I noticed one of my soldiers was missing and not with the group. It was just my luck that the speaker of the event reported he was ready to get started a few minutes early and proceeded to begin seating everyone. As the clock struck 2:59 and the speaker was delivering his open remark, guess who made their grand entrance? You guessed it, my soldier. If you are not familiar with how the military works, let me quickly brief you. Because you are responsible for your soldiers, in the event they mess up, the blame from the higher authorities does not fall on them, it falls on the person in charge, and in this case it was me. Directly after the event, I had to answer to my commanding officers and explain why my soldier was not "on time."

Being human, I was instantly filled with embarrassment and anger because I specifically requested that everyone show up ten minutes before the event was scheduled.

Prior to approaching my soldier, I used the hand method and attempted to look beyond my hand. I put into perspective that not only was my soldier new to the army, but also punctuality may not have been that important to him before joining the army. In his eyes, showing up before the event started, which was at 3:00 p.m., was early. With that being said, I specified that they arrive ten minutes early, and he did not. As a leader, I had to make a choice: do I approach him and ridicule him as my superiors did me, or do I use this incident to mold and groom? Yes, I could yell at him and make him do push-ups (which is routine corrective action in the army), and this may ensure he would show up early out of fear next time—or I could talk to him and educate him on the importance of being punctual. I decided to choose the route of speaking with him, educating him, and ensuring he learned from the experience moving forward. This allowed me to learn more about him and pick his brain to see why he thought disregarding the rules of being ten minutes early was okay. This resulted in a learning moment for both him and me.

Being able to realize that there is more to life than what you choose to focus on will allow you to make decisions that will improve your life and the lives of others as well. Many businesses, marriages, and friendships fail because human beings cannot change the angle to change the picture. If you are this way, don't feel bad. You are one of many, including me at one point. It is natural for humans to focus on what is right in front of our eyes instead of what's beyond what we see or choose to focus on. This is also very relatable to how we feel about our personal achievements and lessons.

There is no such thing as losses in life, but only lessons. I say "lessons" instead of "losses" because we have the opportunity to choose to learn from every situation we are faced with. It is up to us to allow events in our lives to sit us down or show us another path to walk. The choice is always ours.

Let's say you are fired from your job. Most people would be filled with emotions: anger, sadness, grief. However, if you choose to view being fired as a lesson rather than a loss, you will understand that the universe, or whoever you deem as your higher power, chose to shake your cage to free you. Perhaps you have outgrown your job and the only way you are going to progress to something bigger and better is if your circumstances change.

When we are met with resistance at a point in our life, it is not a coincidence. There is no such thing as a coincidence.

A coincidence is just an event that an individual has yet to identify the meaning of.

If you are working toward something and can't seem to get to that personal goal you have set for yourself, all that means is that it's time for you to look beyond your hand. It may be time for you to change your angle to see another part of the picture to understand why you are not meeting that goal fully.

Reflection Notes

ACTION 2

CREATE YOUR OWN BELIEFS & VALUES

Lots of people assume they create their own beliefs and values. In actuality, most of our beliefs and values stem from those that raised us and programming from everything we've observed. Well-known psychologist Sigmund Freud is historically known for his theory that there are three minds: the *conscious mind*, the *unconscious mind*, and the *preconscious mind*, which is known today as the *subconscious mind*.

Think of the subconscious mind as the automatic mind, your second nature; it reacts without you having to think. An example of this is when you ask for a piece of gum. Once you receive the gum, you don't have to think to put it in your mouth, you just do. The unconscious mind can be compared to a database. It's where your memories, feelings, and habits are all stored. The conscious mind is your awareness.

Think of it as if you were learning karate for the first time, slowly going through the motions with the next movement on the forefront of your mind.

Here is an example of the three minds working together. We all have that friend or acquaintance that has a goal of losing weight. They desire to look like the girls in the movies or the guys on the cover of every fitness magazine. However, they never seem to stay committed to eating right or exercising. Is this their fault? Let's take a look. Maybe subconsciously they're eating badly and making excuses for not going to the gym because as a child, they saw skinny kids getting bullied. Or maybe at some point in their life, they saw trusting people resulted in them or someone they knew getting hurt. Subsequently, they keep living this unhealthy lifestyle and adding weight to their body with the unconscious idea that heavier people do not have friends, so them being heavier lowers their chances of them getting close to someone and getting hurt. Consciously, they want to work out and eat healthier, but subconsciously they don't because unconsciously (I dare you to say that five times out loud really fast, haha), they are protecting themself from what they perceive as unsafe territory.

Another example of the conscious, subconscious, and unconscious mind at work is when we are driving. Have you ever driven from work to home and as you pull into your driveway you have no idea how you got there? That was your subconscious mind working with your conscious mind. As mentioned previously, your unconscious mind can be referred to as a database. It stores your patterns and successfully allows your subconscious mind to get you home while you still consciously react to things around you, such as pedestrians, other cars, and traffic lights.

Now that we have identified the differences and relations between the conscious mind, unconscious mind, and subconscious mind and the roles they play, let us dive in to how they affect us. Most, if not all, of our beliefs and what we tend to value in our lives are not chosen by us consciously. An insurmountable amount of grief, hardship, and dissatisfaction stems from our environment and how we were raised. For example, suppose person A grew up in an environment where their family struggled financially. They will unconsciously tend to value money. They may form a belief system that working more than one job to obtain multiple streams of income to ensure financial stability is the way to go. Now let's take a moment to look on the flip side. If person B was raised in a household where their family and friends were financially stable, they might tend to value relationships over money because they did not witness financial struggle. They will likely form a belief system of thinking that jobs don't bring financial freedom, relationships do.

If you're still not convinced on the theory of the conscious mind, unconscious mind, and subconscious mind and how it correlates to what and who we have around us, shaping our beliefs and values, then let's take a look into science. Have you ever heard of *epigenetics*? Epigenetics is the study of how the environment someone is exposed to can trigger how their genes subsequently act. Without getting too technical and putting my Einstein hat on, your genes are made up of deoxyribonucleic acid, also known as DNA. Every human being has DNA from both of their parents. Let's say someone's father was or is addicted to drugs. The child of the father will carry the genes for addictive traits or an addictive personality. This does not mean that the person will be addicted to drugs at some point in their life, but they likely will show addictive traits to something: food, abusive relationships, working, or shopping, to name a few. The question now is, when will the person's addictive traits or personality begin to surface? This is where epigenetics comes into play. If said person is in an environment that causes them stress, the stress hormone can then trigger the addictive gene passed on by the father, activating the cycle of addictive behavior.

In my early twenties, I found myself instantly being disinterested in conversations with younger people and seeking to find holes in their story when they were doing what I perceived to be lecturing. I believed they were too young to know what they were talking about. There were times when I would walk away from the conversation and not remember one thing they said. A good friend of mine brought this to my attention, highlighting my behavior toward younger people. The disappointment he displayed toward my actions caused me to sit back and reflect deeply. Going within, I began searching for the source of why I would disengage and insist on finding holes in conversations with people younger than me. I reflected and realized that if it were someone of my age or older, I would listen with the assumption that they were speaking with more knowledge and experience, and I could learn from them and put myself in a better position financially, mentally, or spiritually. Then it suddenly hit me: this programming stemmed from my upbringing with my parents. I grew up in a Caribbean (Guyanese) household. In Caribbean culture, when an adult is talking, the child stays quiet and has no say so. Although as an adult I am now conscious of why my parents are the way they are, as a child and teenager, I could not identify, understand, or discern this behavior until well into my mid-twenties.

My unconscious mind held on to this behavior that I witnessed and endured. It surfaced subconsciously, negating conversations from individuals younger than me. It took some time for me to realize that I was using the wrong measuring tool for wisdom. I was using *age* as my measuring tool instead of *experience*. I could only imagine how many meaningful and opportunistic conversations I may have missed out on due to this subconscious reaction.

Values are things like principles and qualities we place importance on or desire. Growing up, *The Fresh Prince of Bel-Air*, *The Jeffersons*, and *The Cosby Show* were shows I watched continually that displayed the image of a perfect marriage and family. The father was the breadwinner and protector. The mother, whether she worked or not, cleaned, cooked dinner, and made sure the kids were taken care of. These television shows shaped my values without me even realizing it and later, would challenge my marriage more than I ever could have imagined. But before I dive in, let's break down the word *television*: tell-a-vison! Television tells us or projects a vision onto us. Without us being consciously aware of it, the TV shows, movies, or documentaries we watch project a vision into our unconscious mind. For example, if you frequently watch movies about thugs, you will subconsciously begin to act like one or do everything you can not to become one without consciously trying to. In my case, I was constantly shown a vision of what a "perfect" family is supposed to look like, and I wanted that.

In today's society, it is virtually impossible to reach a level of monetary success without both partners in the household having a stable source of income, unless your last name is Gates, Musk, Bezos, or Buffett. Although my last name does not resemble any of those names, I have done well for myself. I am a successful soldier, speaker, investor, and author. At the same time, my wife is an entrepreneur and holds a master's degree in social work, focusing on the demanding field of substance abuse. With all of this listed, your question must be, "Well, what is the issue?" The answer is, there is no issue. However, I unconsciously put value on a woman cooking, cleaning, and taking care of the family, which was nurtured by what I grew up watching on TV. That caused a constant issue in my marriage. I had to unlearn to relearn. First, I had to identify the source of the issue. Second, I had to unlearn my unconscious programming about wanting a woman to do what society granted a woman should be and do. This allowed me to then create new values and beliefs that have gotten my marriage where it is today. I had to value my wife having a career that didn't allow her to cook and clean every day, but allowed her to be financially independent, which allowed us to reach our goal as a union to be financially independent.

Once we begin to acknowledge that we did not consciously create our own beliefs and values, we get to begin choosing and constructing new ones. Acknowledging that you did not consciously create your own beliefs and values will allow you to isolate and identify the root of the problem. Next, you must stop surrounding yourself with people that negatively influence you and stop placing yourself in environments that will cause unconscious downloads that do not support the way you want to live your life. Once you begin to do these two things, you will begin to witness change.

Reflection Notes

Action 3

Use a Filter

Ten years ago, this chapter would be exclusively based on filtering the physical people around you, but it's not that easy in 2021. With the emergence of social platforms such as Facebook, Instagram, Snapchat, TikTok, and many others, it is just as important to filter those around you virtually. There are currently just over 3.9 billion active users across all social media platforms. In the United States, the average person spends about two to three hours a day scrolling on these platforms. That means, on any given day, a multitude of people is influencing us.

Take a second to think of all the people you currently follow on all of your social media platforms. Most people follow between two hundred and five thousand people on social media but cannot think of two hundred people they actually know in their lives. That indicates that on any given day, you are being influenced by people you don't know. You get a snapshot of their lives, and they begin to influence how you live yours.

Think about your career field. If you haven't discovered your desired career field, think about what you want to be. Is it a doctor? Lawyer? Comedian? CEO of your own business? Now think about how many people you follow that mirror the career field you have chosen. If your answer to that question is not at least 60 percent, then it's time for you to do some filtering. If you intend to become a lawyer or doctor, how is watching the lives of rappers or Instagram models for two to three hours a day helping you? It's not! As pointed out in Action 2, your unconscious mind is a database that's continuously downloading information, information that's influencing your subconscious mind. There's no coincidence that instead of thinking about how to be the best lawyer, doctor, or entrepreneur, all you can seem to think about is the latest song by one of the many rappers whose name starts with Lil. I understand life is about balance. There is no dark without light, hot without cold, or happiness without sadness, but it is up to you to know when the scale is tipping too much to the side that doesn't benefit your desired outcome.

Now that we've begun filtering certain unconscious aspects of our lives that have great impacts, it's time to filter the ones we physically see. There tends to be a major misconception that we should never turn our back on our family. First, we must begin to redefine the word *family*. Most of us have family members we've known our entire lives, yet if we are in a bad situation, they are not the people we would call for help. I use this example because it's not about who we're connected to biologically; instead it's about who's there to help elevate us, support us, and allow us to do the same for them. Many of us tend to put ourselves in predicaments that hinder our current circumstances because we feel the obligation to be loyal to a group of people whose only true connection to us is blood. It's time to begin the practice of learning to protect our energy and livelihood at all costs. We must not be afraid of or shy away from filtering. If the people around you have shown even a small glimpse of not being able to make decisions to better their life, why are you allowing them to hang around you?

Let's use a car as an example. If you're looking for a parking space, you're not going to park next to a beat-up 1999 Oldsmobile. The decision not to park near this car doesn't stem from the make, model, or year of the car, but because of how the owner has cared for it. If the car owner doesn't care about his or her car, you can almost guarantee he or she won't care about yours. You will likely attempt to park near a car that looks as if the owner cares for it, or just find a parking space away from everyone. That is how you should treat your life!

Joining the military allowed me to develop the ability to have a macro view on life that I never had growing up in my neighborhood. It allowed me to move away from my environment, build confidence, have a sense of responsibility, and take pride in having accomplishments. Although I love where I'm from because it helped groom me into the man I am today, I despise going home. The majority of my childhood friends spend most of their days smoking, partying, or getting into fights with people from the neighborhood. Because they're my childhood friends, I used to feel obligated to catch up with them when I came to town. This all changed when one of my "friends" attempted to get me to smoke marijuana with him, even though he knew smoking marijuana is prohibited for all service members. Once I declined, his response was, "Stop being scared. You don't have to go back to work for the next thirty days, and it should be out of your system by then." In this moment I realized I had parked my car next to an Oldsmobile that had not been maintained. If he doesn't care about elevating himself and bettering his life, why would he care about mine and my professional guidelines? So of course I began to distance myself.

It is imperative in life that you begin to place distance between you and those that don't want more for themselves. There is nothing wrong with attempting to help others, but not at the expense of hurting yourself. Most people struggle to elevate further in life because they're trying to take people with them who don't belong with them—ultimately hindering their ability to excel.

The next time you're stuck and can't seem to find out why it's been so hard to get the job you want, start that business, or simply be happy, ask yourself, is it time to filter your life?

Reflection Notes

_____

_____

_____

_____

_____

_____

_____

_____

_____

_____

_____

_____

_____

_____

_____

_____

_____

_____

Reflection Notes

ACTION 4

THE FIVE-FINGER RULE

Have you ever questioned a choice you wanted to make because someone told you it was difficult, suggesting you take what seemed like an easier route to your goal? My question now is, why haven't you questioned if they are even qualified to give you that suggestion? Have they tried what you're striving to accomplish? Have they succeeded at what you're trying to accomplish? If the answer to the last two questions is no, then stop allowing them to question your goals and provide their input on how you'll accomplish them. Most people aren't happy in their relationships, career fields, or overall lives because their happiness is contingent on others' reactions and support.

I created the five-finger rule and implemented it in my daily decision-making because I was tired of allowing people to dictate what I was going to do with my life. I was tired of telling myself no until some else said yes.

At this point, I am sure you are asking yourself, "What in the heck is the five-finger rule?" I am sorry to disappoint, but it literally has to do with your five fingers.

If someone came to you and told you that you don't have five fingers, I am almost positive you'd do two things. First, you'd look confused because maybe they'd mistaken you for someone else. Second, you'd chuckle. What you wouldn't do is look down at your hand to check if you have all five of your fingers. You would do the first two things because you have no doubt in your mind that you have all five of your fingers. You are so certain and confident that you have all of your fingers that it would be comical and borderline bizarre for someone to make this kind of accusation. This is the same way you need to think about any plan or goal you have projected to manifest in your life. You should be so confident in your abilities, your work ethic, and the undaunting work of the universe that it becomes comical when someone even thinks about questioning your goals.

Before I decided to put my all into helping others mentally detox and reprogram their minds, I was told by a co-worker that I should look into doing something else. He told me I wasn't old enough to give anyone advice, and no one would pay to have me speak to them. That short conversation sent me down a spiral of thoughts: "Is he right? What if people can't relate to me? Maybe I shouldn't take this as seriously and have a plan B." It wasn't until I decided that my plan B would be to make my plan A work that I saw change. I confidently decided my messages would be received by those who needed to hear them and exactly when they needed to. I began to believe that I did have experiences people could learn from, and I also have a unique way of demonstrating conviction within my messages that would allow the listener to receive them. Here I am, six years later, an author and public speaker who has been on many stages. I can confidently say that I have changed the lives of many by using my voice. If I would have believed what my co-worker told me, I would have limited myself and cheated countless others out of a message they needed to get them through the day.

When you believe in yourself, you can't be afraid to take a risk. Risk is what separates those that want from those that have. When you are truly prepared and willing to do whatever it takes to reach your goals, risk becomes necessary. The only way for you to reach the other side of the bridge is to jump. When you don't believe in yourself, you begin to think, "If I jump, I can fall," but those that believe in themselves start to think, "If I don't jump, I can't fly."

Sometimes the person we need to use the five-finger rule on is ourselves. One of our biggest doubters is within. You cannot manifest something in your life if you don't believe you already have it. A big misconception of manifestation is that we are trying to attain something.

Manifestation is about knowing deep within that you already have it but have yet to claim and work toward it. What is meant for you is already yours and will never pass you by.

It is imperative not to allow someone who has never walked in your shoes to tell you where you are going. Many people hate to see others reach their maximum potential and work toward their goals because it is a continuous reminder of how they may have given up on theirs. The five-finger rule functions as a reminder to push forward no matter what others think. At the end of the day, all that matters is what you think about yourself and your abilities. Remember, if Walt Disney, Steve Jobs, and Jeff Bezos all listened to others' opinions, they probably never would have made it out of their garages where they all started. We would never have gotten the most popular cellular device of the twenty-first century, the most popular theme park in the world, and the world's largest online retail provider. So the next time someone doubts you and assumes that you don't have what it takes to reach the goals you've set for yourself, I want you to ask yourself in confidence or out loud, "Do I have five fingers?"

Reflection Notes

Reflection Notes

ACTION 5

MEDITATE

The last and final action I implemented in my life was meditation. Don't close the book just yet. I know you're thinking, "Meditation! What does that have to do with me becoming successful in any aspect of my life?" Research shows that individuals have an average of over six thousand thoughts a day! This means even when we're not engaged in a conversation with another person, our mind is still working because it is continuously communicating with the most important person in our lives: us!

Most people believe the only way to meditate is to sit on the floor with your legs crossed as we did in preschool during quiet time, touching your fingers together and closing your eyes. Although that is the most popular form of meditation in Eastern and modern Western civilization, there are other ways to meditate. Meditation is simply allowing yourself to be present.

It is not worrying about what happened in the past or thinking about what can happen in the future, but rather accepting and being present with who and where we are in this second.

Reading your favorite novel, dancing or singing along to your favorite song, and even going for a light jog are all different forms of meditation. All of these activities have something in common: they allow you to escape from the thoughts of the past or future. When you're reading your favorite mystery novel, you become consumed with the characters and storyline. When you're singing or dancing to your favorite song, you're not thinking at all; you're just allowing the melody and vibrations of the music to feed your soul and move your feet. When you're out on a jog, you're focusing on your breathing. You're not thinking about what you're going to eat later or why you didn't get that promotion at work you feel you deserved. You focus on controlling your breathing and block out all the mental noise.

Being a soldier, husband, speaker, podcast host, real estate investor, and proud dog dad, it's safe to say that finding time to center myself and become present is very important. Before I started to incorporate meditation into my daily routine, I would often find myself burned out. At first, I thought that continuously working and giving my time to others would help me achieve my goals, but it was quite the opposite. I wasn't able to give my all because I was running off of an oversaturated and exhausted mind. Once I found the secret to this glorious thing called meditation, doors began to open up for me that I had no clue were even there. I was able to give my mind a break, and in turn, I was able to do more.

Your brain is a muscle. Imagine going to the gym daily, for hours at a time, and pushing yourself to your maximum while you're there. You would never be able to reach your full potential. There's a reason why the most famous bodybuilders in the world don't work on biceps every day. They usually work on different muscle groups at a time. Why? Because they're aware that an exhausted muscle will never allow them to get to the level they are aiming for. The mind is the same way. You have to find time to allow your mind to relax, and as a result, it will begin to work at an optimal level.

When choosing your activity, you must make sure the selected activity will allow you to vibrate at a high frequency. Frequencies are measured on a wide range of emotions. These emotions range from shame, which is the lowest frequency you can vibrate on, all the way to enlightenment, which is the highest frequency you can vibrate on. You want to stay away from the frequencies at the bottom and attempt to vibrate in the middle and upward.

Everyone has their own preferred activity that allows them to tap into a meditative state. However, you must choose an activity that is healthy and beneficial to your life and unconscious mind. I'm sorry to tell all my gamers out there, but playing shooting games is not an activity I recommend.

Listening to music that degrades women or has profanity in every other sentence is also not beneficial.

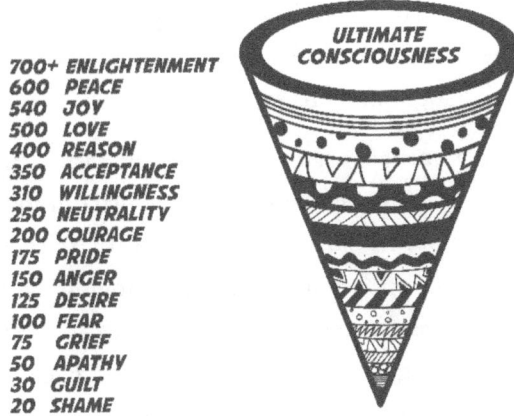

700+ ENLIGHTENMENT
600 PEACE
540 JOY
500 LOVE
400 REASON
350 ACCEPTANCE
310 WILLINGNESS
250 NEUTRALITY
200 COURAGE
175 PRIDE
150 ANGER
125 DESIRE
100 FEAR
75 GRIEF
50 APATHY
30 GUILT
20 SHAME

ULTIMATE CONSCIOUSNESS

Playing shooter games or listening to low-vibrational music will unconsciously begin to reprogram your brain, affecting your ability to discern, and can possibly cause depression.

If you're a business owner or someone that relies heavily on your creative ability, meditation could possibly give you a mental edge over others in your field. It's been said that well-revered artists such as Vincent van Gogh, known for his painting *The Starry Night*, and Leonardo Da Vinci, known for his painting *Mona Lisa*, both were known for tapping into a meditative state when painting. They mastered the ability to block out the world and focus on the present. This skill gave them the mental edge required to create their prominent paintings that can never be replicated.

If having a mental edge over your peers isn't enough to convince you that meditation is an action that can change your life for the better, how about science? In today's society everything is fast-paced; here today, gone tomorrow. Having a high-tempo lifestyle can cause an individual a great deal of stress. Stress triggers a hormone called *cortisol*. Excess amounts of cortisol into your bloodstream can result in neurological effects such as fatigue, memory loss, and most commonly, depression. Meditation has been shown to decrease the amount of cortisol released and can help overall brain function. Implementing this practice into your life will undoubtedly give you noticeable results, but it is up to you to begin.

Reflection Notes

THE ROUNDUP

O nce you've implemented these five actions in your life, you will begin to see things fall into place. You don't need to rush to complete any of these actions, and you don't have to do them in any particular order. It's up to you to decide which action you will take first. By choosing to read this book, you are showing your willingness to unlearn to relearn. In life, the goal is not perfection, but executing the actions outlined in this book will allow you to reach a level of success you have yet to reach financially, emotionally, and in all other aspects of your life.

These actions have helped improve my marriage, leadership abilities, businesses, and the way I feel about myself. My goal was to share them to help readers excel in anything they are trying to pursue. Now that you know these actions, it's time for you to act.

DAILY AFFIRMATIONS

- *I AM WHAT I THINK OF MYSELF.*
- *I AM WORTHY.*
- *I FORGIVE.*
- *I AM LOVED.*
- *I AM BLESSED.*
- *I AM CONFIDENT.*
- *I AM BEAUTIFUL.*
- *I AM COURAGEOUS.*
- *I AM ATTRACTING ABUNDANCE.*
- *I AM WEALTHY PHYSICALLY AND SPIRITUALLY.*
- *I AM ROYALTY.*
- *I AM ONE.*
- *I AM.*

Made in United States
Cleveland, OH
07 December 2024